Sheringham clock tower was built as a reservoir; it had a horse trough on one wall and a tap on another – one of just two public sources of water in the town for anyone who did not have their own well. The fountain and reservoir depicted on the front cover of this booklet served a similar purpose in Upper Sheringham.

Foreword

Sheringham is a town steeped in history. From humble beginnings it has developed into a residential haven and popular holiday resort. Along the way it has been peopled by generations of those who have lived in the shadow of the unpredictable North Sea, those who have respected it for the rich harvests it can provide, those who have fought it in the name of the lifeboat service and those who have lost loved ones to it.

Gone is the once thriving fishing industry. Gone are the unforgettable characters who peopled its streets. Gone, too, are many of its once notable buildings. 'Progress' has a lot to answer for.

A book such as this can only scratch the surface to reveal something of what has gone before. Memories are fallible and it is sometimes difficult to record exactly what happened only a couple of generations ago.

It is hoped that the reader will find some items of interest in this condensed story of the history and development of Sheringham. The author will always be interested to hear from anyone who can contribute in any way to our knowledge and understanding of the town's history.

5 Abbey Road, Sheringham NR26 8HH **Peter Brooks**

Early history

Although it is the town of Sheringham which today is the centre of attraction, it is to the village of Upper Sheringham, 1½ miles inland, that we must look in order to start our story.

In 1940, when gold coins were found on the beach between Sheringham and Weybourne, they were thought to have belonged to a Gaulish tribe which inhabited the area during the first century BC. A Roman kiln and pottery have been found in Upper Sheringham; there is a tumulus at Howe's Hill; 'shrieking pits', used for smelting iron ore, can still be seen along the Cromer Ridge; and we know that this stretch of coast was successively attacked and plundered by the Angles, Saxons and Vikings. The more recent discovery at Beeston Regis of an axe, spearheads and pottery dating back to the 9th century BC is also proof of very early occupation. Certainly the high ground of the Ridge offered, and still does, a wonderful vantage point from which would-be invaders could readily be seen, and on which beacons could be lit to warn of impending danger.

It is not until the Domesday Book of 1086 that we learn of the existence of a church at Upper Sheringham, then known as Silingham and later Siringham (1172) and Schyringham (1291). However spelt, the derivation is Scandinavian and denotes the home of Scira's people, so obviously not all those early raiders returned home!

Beeston Priory, about 1905.

The parish was on a pilgrimage route to Walsingham and in 1197 an Augustinian Priory was established at Beeston Regis to augment that already existing at Weybourne. The priors were subsequently accused of committing 'manifest sins' and of indulging in 'vicious carnal and abominable living' and after earlier, unsuccessful, attempts to move them the Priory was eventually suppressed in June 1539. Ruined parts of the Priory and its church can still be seen and they are sufficient to give us some idea of the importance of this once notable building, both in the local community and as a place of hospitality to travellers. In fact

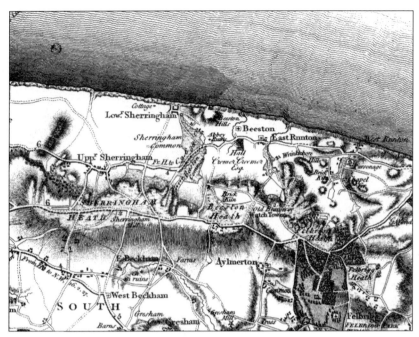

Sheringham and its vicinity, from Faden's map published in 1797. Upper Sheringham has a spread of houses, and Lower Sheringham just a small grouping.

the existence of the Priory gave Beeston an importance superior to the village of Sheringham and it was not until the 17th century that the latter was to become the dominant centre in the area.

Inevitably the history of this small part of Britain is inextricably linked with the rolling sea on its doorstep. The relationship has dominated the growth of the town of Sheringham at the expense of Upper Sheringham, and has woven the very fabric, not only of the town, but of the men and women who have given it life and character.

The men of the original community in Upper Sheringham sought their livings from the sea, launching their boats from the slopes of Sheringham Hythe, some 1½ miles west of the present town and in line with the sixth green on the golf course. It was here too, in later years, that a lifeboat house was to stand.

But it was the newly established community of Lower Sheringham, with its freshwater beck and gentle slope to the beach, that grew in importance. As the years slipped by rough wooden buildings were replaced by flint and pebble-walled cottages and soon blacksmiths, net-makers, rope-spinners, tanners and shopkeepers were attracted to the parish to make it self-sufficient. Fish merchants soon established themselves and in 1358 they were specifically empowered, provided that other traders were not inconvenienced and the price of fish did not rise, to buy fish at the flourishing nearby port of Blakeney. A further concession came in 1374 when local fishermen were exempted from paying a subsidy of 6*d* in the pound on the catches. It was still Upper Sheringham, however, that dominated, for this was the home of the parish church, and was to continue to be so until 1953 when St Peter's became the parish church for Sheringham town.

All Saints, Upper Sheringham, was built during the middle to late 14th century, the tower, chancel and font surviving from that period. The size of the churchyard is evidence of a much larger population than today and the numerous memorials to those lost at sea stand as a silent testimony. The village sign shows the first lifeboat, the *Augusta*, pulling for the shore and two mermaids are prominent. Why mermaids? They come from the delightful legend that tells us of the little mermaid who came to the north door of the church while a service was in progress. The Beadle, horrified, cried out 'Git yew arn owt. We carn't hev noo marmeards in hare!' He slammed the door in her face, but she was a very determined little creature and when no one was looking she crept in and seated herself on the outside edge of the pew nearest the door. She is still there today, in company with the sailing ships carved into the pew seats by generations of young boys with their minds more on the challenges of life to come than the sermon being preached.

Boats and a harbour

During the early part of the 16th century a tax of 4*d* was levied on all boats working in and out of Sheringham. Later a system of 'doles' was introduced in which, following the completion of a fishing trip, the net profit, after deducting all operating costs, was distributed in five parts: one to pay all legal expenses, one to provide 'Christ's Dole' for the parson, and one part each for the port commissioners, the crew and the owner.

Records of the number and type of boats sailing from Sheringham are sparse. In 1580 two vessels were attributed to the town, the 30-ton *Peter* owned by William Allison and the 14-ton *John* owned by Edmund Hooke. By 1591 the number had grown to 17 full-time and five part-time boats.

There must have been considerable local expertise in the building of boats, for both the Upcher lifeboats were built in the town. The principal craftsmen were Henry Lown and Lewis (Buffalo) Emery; the latter built the *Henry Ramey Upcher* lifeboat which can be seen in its shed at the top of the Fishermen's Gangway. The Emery family built boats until 1957 and then operated a repair business until 1980, their former boat-building shed on Lifeboat Plain now virtually unrecognisable having been converted to residential use. All their boats were built 'by eye' with a complete absence of instruments and drawings. When Henry Lown

4

retired, a former apprentice, John Johnson, took the business over and built the business up to rival that of the Emerys. Both worked entirely without plans and although the exact number of boats built by these craftsmen is not known it has to be around the 200 mark, many of them still in use along the North Norfolk coast. Other local boatbuilders included Tom Boxall who carried on his business in Station Road (more or less opposite Melbourne Road) and Robert Sunman of Upper Sheringham who built the *Augusta* lifeboat.

The small boats built by Emery and Lown were designed for working off the kind of sloping beaches found at Sheringham. Double-ended for ease of handling and beaching, they were open with no decking and an average length of 19 feet. With a width of about seven feet and a depth of just over three feet they

Harold and Reggie Emery (above, in their boat-building shed in 1952) made boats like the ones pictured below (which have been pulled up Beach Road in 1904); they are of traditional north Norfolk style, double-ended and clinker built with 'orrucks' and a simple dipping lugsail.

Sheringham fishermen, probably about 1890, with baskets of whelks.

handled well in rough seas and, before the introduction of engines, were powered by a sail made from about 35 yards of heavy calico or duck, tanned to a deep brown, and set to an 18-foot mast.

No longer do we see the luggers, or Great Boats, so common in the 1880s, the last of which were seen offshore in 1907. During the 1860s there were about 30 of these boats owned by Sheringham fishermen. Mostly built by Beechings of Great Yarmouth (because of their similarity to the Yarmouth drifters) at a cost of around £300 each, they had a crew of upwards of a dozen men and spent their time searching for crabs, herring, mackerel and cod off the Yorkshire and Lincolnshire coasts as well as with the herring drifters operating out of Lowestoft and Great Yarmouth. They took their crab boats with them, securely fastened to the decks, and many youngsters of 10 and 12 years of age got their first taste of a fisherman's life as they accompanied their fathers and brothers on these extended trips. The Yorkshire crabs were lighter in colour than their Sheringham counterparts and to this day light brown crabs are known as 'Yorkshiremen'. Because of their size these boats could not be hauled onto the beach for safety and so they returned only two or three times a year before lying up at Blakeney or Wells, or exchanging their long lines and crab pots for drift-nets prior to the autumnal herring fishing. At such times fleets of these magnificent sailing craft could be seen off the centre beach. In October 1880 eight of them were caught in a furious storm. As the crews attempted to get under way the *Gleaner* overturned, to be washed ashore at Beeston; her crew of 11, skippered by George 'Coaches' Craske, were lost.

Whelking was also a major industry in the town and during the 1920s and 1930s Sheringham was a major supplier to London and Midland markets, with boiling coppers situated in many parts of the town. The industry is remembered in the name 'Whelkcoppers' given to the large house on the western promenade close to the Fishermen's Slipway. Local people recall the thick black smoke that used to pour from the copper chimneys on its western end. Although the price plummetted to 1*s* 3*d* a wash (the Sheringham equivalent to one third of a hundredweight) during the mid-1920s, it picked up again, only for the trade to die out during the period 1937–39 when anti-aircraft gunnery practice from Weybourne Camp made fishing of the grounds impossible. The importance of the trade to the town was confirmed by the local football team who wore a golden whelk on the pocket of their shirts.

Before the fishermen began to market their own catches (about 1925) beach auctions were a colourful and noisy aspect of local life. They continued until the 1930s and local people can recall box upon box of cod, skate, mackerel and herring being laid out on the west gangway, with merchants bidding against a backcloth of rolling waves, the cry of wheeling gulls and the hum of animated conversation.

The fish buyer (in the bowler hat) makes his purchases. The photo is dated about 1895.

Despite all this activity Sheringham never became a trading port, although there was a small traffic in coal. Henry Ramey Upcher owned two schooners which used to bring coal down from the North East to be unloaded into carts at low tide, a practice which continued up to the beginning of the twentieth century. The coalyard was next to the Crown Inn and the price was about a shilling a hundredweight.

Communities such as Sheringham began to realise they were at a great disadvantage in not possessing sheltered harbourages such as existed at Cley and Blakeney, and attempts were made to overcome the problem of their exposed position by building an artificial harbour. By 1578 the townships of Beeston and Sheringham had 'fallen into sooche great ruyne and decays' that three local justices were moved to petition the Crown to make a 'generous provision' so that a harbour might be constructed. Five years later, on 16th February 1583, Queen Elizabeth issued letters patent authorising Robert Kirke, William Garter and Roger Sturgeon to construct a pier, the money to be raised by fines imposed for seven years on the flax and hemp growers of Norfolk and Suffolk.

The plan was to construct a harbour encompassing some 4.5 acres, a daunting task even by modern standards. Work started on 5th April of the same year on

A coal ship unloads its cargo on the beach. The trade in coal from the East Durham coalfield thrived in the middle of the 19th century but died with the coming of the railways.

a 260-foot-long western pier and it says something for the determination of the three men that this was completed by August of the following year. Work immediately started on an eastern pier some 180 feet in length, this being completed in October 1585. Construction was of oak piles infilled with stone and the records show that the contractors were paid 2*s* 6*d* and the workmen 1*s* 2*d* a day for their labours. The harbour did not survive for any length of time. It is worth recording that even with all the modern equipment of today progress could hardly have been better, and many will recall the occasion when, in 1961, contractors working on the town's sea defences lost much equipment during a severe storm.

Fears of invasion

There is a rhyme that goes

> *He who would old England win*
> *must at Weybourne Hope begin.*

This is because of the very deep water just off-shore and its truth is reflected in the fact that during the Second World War there was a heavy gun emplacement on Skelding Hill and large concentrations of troops in the area ready to repel any invasion attempt. In 1588 the threat was from the Spanish Armada and defensive measures included cutting the cliffs to a defined slope, blocking up the passage to the sea with a parapet 'when necessary', and digging trenches on Sheringham (Beeston) Heath, a precaution repeated during the First World War. During the reign of Charles I two regiments were stationed in the area and charged to be ready 'upon one houre's warninge'. Failure to achieve this was 'at their uttmost perill'. The troops were quartered in houses in the town and guards were set at night to keep a sea watch.

In July 1673, fearful of an invasion by the Dutch, the townspeople petitioned the Lord Lieutenant, complaining they had only one gun with a broken carriage and four muskets with no powder or shot. They asked for four or five muskets, 50 pounds of powder and 50 pounds of bullets. Almost immediately they were granted 6 muskets and all the powder and bullets requested for the defence of Sheringham Hythe, 'and not otherwise'. The ancient gun to be seen at the top of Gun Street is thought to be the one mentioned in the petition, although it could date from the time of the Spanish Armada in 1588, when plans were drawn up for a fort at Weybourne. A contemporary drawing depicts the presence of such a gun as part of the defences at the Old Hythe.

Fear of invasion was still strong in 1803 when a group of merchantmen in convoy were mistaken for a French invasion fleet, and the King ordered a scorched earth policy should any landing be made by French forces. It is also known that troops were stationed along Weybourne cliffs during 1814–15 ready to repel another feared French invasion.

The poor and needy

The poor and needy of years ago had to rely very much on the charity of others. However, in a community like Sheringham, with its fiercely independent fisher-folk, there were many who would rather struggle on at starvation level than accept help from outside their family. Nevertheless, there were several poor people in the parish unable to pay their taxes and needing goods as well as money if they were to survive.

In 1791 there were 20 souls in Upper Sheringham and seven in Lower Sheringham receiving weekly payments of between 6d and 4s, these comprising 22 women, two men and three girls. Sixteen had their rates remitted; at other times, parishioners had shoes and clothing provided, medical care given, were shaved at the parish's expense, given a coat at Christmas, provided with tools and equipment to enable them to take up or follow a trade, or were given grain for bread making.

Sheringham Park, home of the Upcher family whose gifts benefited many poor people in Sheringham as well as the lifeboat service.

The local Overseer was a very busy man for, apart from administering to the poor, he was also responsible for clearing the Beck, mending the roads, ditching, maintaining watercourses and a host of other duties essential to everyday life. The Town Book records that the stocks, on the site of what is now the Clock Tower, were repaired at a cost of 1*s* and a lock fixed at a cost of 3½*d*. The pillory was also sited here and older residents can recall their parents speaking of other stocks and a pillory at Beeston, between the Dunstable Arms public house and the Common. The local mole-catcher was paid £2 a quarter and the Overseer was also responsible for maintaining the House of Industry at Upper Sheringham. This was built in 1805 opposite All Saints church to accommodate 150 old and infirm paupers. It was provided by a co-operative effort between Aldborough, Aylmerton, Beeston Regis, Cromer, East Beckham, Felbrigg, Gresham, Runton and Sheringham. It was in regular use up until 1850 when a new Union House was built at West Beckham, this becoming known locally as 'Beckham Palace'.

Throughout their presence in Sheringham the Upcher family were generous benefactors to the locals, especially the fishermen, starting in 1812 when Abbot Upcher bought Sheringham Hall estate and engaged Humphrey Repton to build his new home. His son, Henry Ramey Upcher, owned the estate for 73 years and it was his mother, Charlotte, who gave the town its first lifeboat, its first allotments and a Sunday School for boys; she also set up a branch of the Bible Society, established soup kitchens in times of hardship for the fishermen, and lent them money so that they could buy their own boats.

But it was not just the men who laboured hard. Life was tough for the women too, with husbands whose next trip could be their last. Generally better educated

11

Littles and Wests pose for a photograph: old Teddy 'Fiddy' West, Walter 'Pongo' Little, young Robert Rufus West, young Walter Little and young Teddy 'Fiddy' West.

than their menfolk, they adopted the role of family banker and taught their children the rudiments of reading, writing and elementary arithmetic in the small, cramped cottages with no modern amenities. The women had large families to cater for and were active in mending nets, hanging them out to dry, preparing bait and keeping their menfolk in ganseys, all of which did not leave much free time. Ganseys were close-fitting jerseys in blue fishermen's yarn (but all wool for the Sunday best) knitted in the round and forming an essential part of a fisherman's dress. A competent knitter could complete one in about two weeks and at the end of the 19th century they cost about 4s each to make. Families tended to have their own distinctive pattern and this practice even extended, in some cases, to whole communities. In such cases the patterns could be used as a means of identification for those fishermen lost at sea and washed ashore far from their home town.

The present 'P and P Charity' amalgamates two ancient charities: first, the 'Ploughlet' charity (formerly known as the Poor's Land Charity), which originally comprised pieces of land called the Town Lands and Town Yards, believed to have been bought out of money made in whaling expeditions. They were superseded in 1811 when the Charity Commissioners, under the Sheringham Inclosure Act, granted other lands in lieu. These have now been sold and investments provide money to give relief to parishioners in the North and South Wards of Shering-

Once the catch had been made, Mr Craske, the fish dealer, could set off on his rounds.

ham and in Upper Sheringham. Second, the 'Poor's Allotments' charity, based on two pieces of land, one comprising 13.29 acres adjoining Sheringham Common, the other 19.8 acres let to the Woodland Caravan Site in Upper Sheringham. The poor were originally allowed to cut furze and flags but this practice has long since lapsed and today the income and investments benefit local folk.

Hooke's Charity derives its name from land purchased from money bequeathed by Edmund Hooke in 1715, although today's beneficiaries are more indebted to the generous provision of an anonymous donor who probably predates Hooke. Rent from the remaining land, plus investments, benefit recipients in the ancient ecclesiastical parish of Beeston Regis, which includes the Beeston Ward of Sheringham.

Cooke's, Goate's and the Wheat charities currently benefit residents in Upper Sheringham, mostly widows, who receive a combined contribution from the three charities. The former gets its revenue from land at High Kelling and the wishes of John Cooke, by his will of 1662, are still observed in that special sermons are preached in the church twice a year prior to the distribution of the charity.

Money for Goate's charity comes from the Lord of the Manor who owns property formerly belonging to John Goate, while the Wheat charity derives from the value of seven pecks of wheat given by the Lord of the Manor in lieu of actual goods.

A more modern charitable trust is that of Lilian Armitage, set up in 1967, which, through income from investments, contributes to the upkeep and relief of elderly ladies in Norwich and Sheringham and their immediate neighbourhoods; the money can be used to pay fees for nursing and residential homes or the making of grants to the homes themselves.

It is perhaps worth recording that it still remains a problem for the various Trustees to find people who are in need and who qualify for help from the various charities. Many are too proud to come forward and ask for help, while others believe the charities do not apply to them.

In 1801 the population of Sheringham was 392, Upper Town still dominating the scene with a shop, three shoemakers and a beerhouse, the Red Lion. Lower Sheringham was still no more than a collection of cottages near the beach, although future development was foreshadowed in the three shops, three shoemakers and five fish-curers who had set up in business. The remains of a chapel dedicated to St Nicholas were to be seen on a site in what is now Wyndham Street (it was the headquarters of the Guild of St Nicholas, an early form of our modern friendly society) and today the site is commemorated by a plaque on the building at the corner with Weston Street. An infant school, founded by Mrs Upcher, offered education to some 60 children and there was a coastguard presence of an officer and six men.

'Go Father' West with crab pots on the beach at Sheringham. Crab pots like these were introduced to the north Norfolk coast in the 1870s.

Nicknames

Not only were there large families but it was common for fathers and sons to have the same christian name, a practice well illustrated by the fact that at one time there were 14 Henry Grices living in Beeston Road! Nicknames were, therefore, an essential form of identification. While some are fairly obvious, as in the case of the West family where a descending order of 'Old Downtide', 'Young Downtide', 'Boy Downtide' and 'Little Downtide' can be found, others are more obscure and associated with physical characteristics, events connected with the various individuals or with personal preferences and idiosyncrasies. The Grice family, for example, can boast men carrying such nicknames as 'Butter-balls', 'King Kong', 'Lally' and 'To Ro Ro Bomshey'. The West family, apart from 'Downtide', can number 'Joyful', 'Nuts', 'Paris', 'Squinter' and 'Teapot' among their titles, while the Pegg family can lay claim to 'Fatty', 'Gay Lad', 'Go Father' (from a young child's difficulty in mastering 'Grandfather'), 'Nimshy', 'Old Gulley', 'Young Gulley' and 'Young Blooming' among their names.

White's directory for 1836 records that Lower Sheringham possessed 'a considerable fishing station, having six curing houses, 26 herring boats and a number of smaller fishing boats'. Cod, skate, whiting, crabs and lobster were plentiful, with great quantities of the latter being sent to London 'by vessels which take the fish from the boats while at sea'. The writer of the time was moved to point out that 'the view of the ocean, peopled with fishermen, or variegated with fleets of colliers, is truly sublime, whilst a peep down the high and rugged cliffs is enough to strike a stranger with horror, though the farmers often plough to the very brink'.

Looking east along the clifftops early in the 20th century, with the cliffs in their natural condition. In the background, the sea has yet to claim the last part of the second of Beeston's two hills.

The fountain and church at Upper Sheringham.

Period of discovery

By 1841 the population of Sheringham had grown to 1,134, it being recorded that 50 fishermen were absent when the census was taken. The total included 70 inmates of the House of Industry which, after considerable alterations, now offered accommodation for 100 residents. Four years later all the fish-curers were still in business and an additional shoe-maker had joined the existing six, so that there were four in Upper Sheringham and three in Lower. There were also ten farmers recorded as making a living from the land, only two of these being in Lower Sheringham. One farm was known as Manor House Farm and was on the site of what is now the Morris Street car park, and the other was known as the Piggeries in what is now Co-operative Street.

The reservoir at Upper Sheringham was erected in 1814 to supply water to the village and this continued as the only public source until mains water became available in the late 1950s. The water supply to Lower Sheringham was improved in 1862 at a cost of £220 when it was piped from the spring to a reservoir at the newly-built Clock Tower, to which women went with buckets, often carried from their shoulders in the manner of milkmaids. An animals' drinking trough was also provided. There was also a sunken, open pit of water at a place known as 'The Polk', approached by steps and situated at the lower end of the High Street near the New Wine Church 'drop-in' centre. It was not until the 1890s that the Sheringham Gas and Water Company was to supply the growing community of Lower Sheringham, and mains sewers laid.

The High Street, Lower Sheringham, in 1862.

In 1864 there were three bakers, three blacksmiths and a tailor in Upper Sheringham, while Lower Sheringham could now boast a post office, four taverns (the Crown, the Dunstable Arms, the Lobster and the Windham Arms), two shoemakers, two tailors and the boat-building firms of Emery and Lown.

Beeston Regis had grown to 196 inhabitants with a school, built in 1836 by Samuel Hoare and supported by his widow. The parish church of All Saints, with nave and chancel dating from the 13th century, was thoroughly restored in 1867 and a local brickworks, the remains of which can be traced on sites near the Beck and in Briton's Lane, were to supply much-needed materials for the building boom to come. The 1886 Ordnance Survey sheet for Sheringham also shows a brickyard, kiln and clay pit about half-way down what is now Church Street.

Kelly's 1875 directory of Norfolk tells us there were 200 boats at Sheringham, 23 of them being 'large and fitted for deep-sea fishing'. The population had grown slowly to 1,250 and civilisation had arrived in the form of a money order office and savings bank, hairdresser, auctioneer and cabinet-maker. The main school was still in Upper Town but the once close-knit and very parochial life of the community was giving way in the face of pressures from the outside world.

By this time visitors, many of them crowded out from Cromer, were discovering the quiet charm of the twin villages of Upper and Lower Sheringham. The extension of the Midland and Great Northern Railway joint branch line from Kings Lynn and Norwich via Melton Constable to the new station on 16th June 1887 marked the end of an era and transition into a developers' paradise with new

Sheringham station and goods yard in its heyday, when trains ran through from the east midlands.

roads, houses and hotels being built at a remarkable pace. This transition is well illustrated by the sentiment, expressed in 1896, that Lower Sheringham 'is now much-frequented as a holiday resort and on account of the increasing number of visitors a large number of private houses have been erected and fine hotels opened between the railway station and the golf links'.

In July 1906 a connection was made, via Cromer, with the Great Eastern Railway to give a direct link with King's Cross and Liverpool Street, the journey taking 3 hours and 13 minutes. A former stationmaster has recalled as many as 64 trains a day steaming in and out of Sheringham station, many of them with special wagons to bring the carriages, landaus and horses which accompanied those coming to stay in the town. When Cromer High station closed in 1954 Sheringham became the terminus for such famous trains as *The Norfolkman* and *The Broadsman*.

Diesel trains were introduced in 1956 and the line to Holt and Melton Constable was closed in April 1964. Goods train services to the town were discontinued in December the same year and Sheringham station closed on 2nd June 1967, an unmanned halt being provided in lieu. On the same day the station site was handed over to the Midland and Great Northern Joint Railway Society (now the North Norfolk Railway Company). An application by British Rail in 1967 to eliminate all train services between Norwich and Sheringham was rejected by the Minister of Transport. Memories of steam survive in the operation of the North Norfolk Railway, who took over the former British Rail line from Sheringham to Weybourne and have since extended it to Holt where a new station has been built.

There is, therefore, some five and a half miles of attractive countryside, much of it within sight of the sea, to be enjoyed on a real steam train trip.

Lodgings in the town are listed for the first time in White's directory of 1883 and a Cromer businessman, James Francis – ironmonger, oil, colorman and cutch merchant – had opened a branch shop in Lower Sheringham. The population of the town was now, surprisingly, down to 1,159 with 23 large and 'about 150 small' boats working from the beach. The Golf Club opened in 1892 as a nine-hole course, extension to 18 holes being completed in July 1898.

The introduction of businessmen from Cromer is interesting for there had always been great rivalry between the two towns, not simply between the fishermen but the inhabitants generally. The local football team, the 'Shannocks' (a name taken from the old 'Shanny', meaning a wild and reckless people, but more recently denoting someone born in Sheringham of Sheringham parents) were renowned for their hard tackling. Both players and spectators can recall occasions when teams have had to be escorted off the field, visiting buses have been stoned and many a bruise has arisen from activities after the matches were officially over! When, at the time of local government reorganisation in 1974, there was a suggestion that the two towns combine in a new coastal authority there were

The Sheringham school football team of season 1934–35. Headmaster Sidney Day is back right.

many letters, both to the local press and the two Urban District Councils, from correspondents deploring such a move and implying that it would be a retrograde step if either of the two communities had to associate with the other!

Bad feelings were certainly generated in 1875 when, during the hearing in Cromer of an investigation into the crab and lobster fisheries of Norfolk by Frank Buckland, Inspector of Salmon Fisheries, Cromer fishermen alleged that while they returned immature shellfish to the sea their counterparts at Sheringham did not, thereby contributing to the decline in the trade. The trade in crabs and lobsters represented the principal industry of the area and 'was of immense importance to the inhabitants'. Such concern was, therefore, understandable particularly when, in evidence, it was stated that the trade had 'fallen off and become impoverished in the last few years to an alarming degree'. Mr Nightingale, a fish merchant of Sheringham, was moved to state 'that at Sheringham at least 28,800 undersized crabs worth barely one farthing each were brought ashore and sold in the course of one day'.

At that time 50 boats fished for crabs from Cromer and about 100 from Sher-

Looking west from Lifeboat Plain, late 19th century. The large number of boats on the beach indicates how many families depended on fishing.

ingham, and witnesses said that whereas they could previously earn around £3 a week, at the time of the hearing they were lucky if their income exceeded £1 per week.

Buckland's report led to the passing of legislation which provided for minimum sizes of shellfish to be caught. (Current legislation requires a minimum landing size for both crabs and lobsters, a carapace width of 115 mm for the former and an 87 mm carapace length for the latter.) This was a move opposed by the Sheringham fishermen who believed that the imposition of the larger sizes would adversely affect their trade. In a deputation to their local MP they said there were more lobsters caught offshore at Sheringham than anywhere else along the coast from Yorkshire to Sussex and in 1949 some 29,182 were landed at Sheringham. They were sold at 2s 6d per pound.

Chapels and churches

By 1896 the church of St Peter's was being built at a cost of £8,000 to replace the Church Mission Chapel which was connected with All Saints of Upper Sheringham, although it was the latter which continued as the town's parish church until 1953 when St Peter's assumed the premier status. Many people from 'Lower' Sheringham are therefore buried in Upper Town churchyard. Coffins were carried the mile or so on the shoulders of family, friends and professional undertakers and, in accordance with custom, a black pall covered not just the coffin but also the heads of the bearers so that they could see only the legs of those in front.

The Wesleyans are believed to have been the first nonconformist group to establish themselves in Sheringham with a chapel in Upper Sheringham in 1826. A Primitive Methodist chapel was built in Lower Sheringham in 1844 (on the site of the present telephone exchange in New Road). This was replaced in 1882 by a larger chapel in Station Road, which in turn was demolished in 1966 for site redevelopment. The Free Methodists built a chapel in Beeston Road in 1859 (later called the United Methodist Church) and this was closed and converted into flats in 1968. St Andrew's Methodist church, built the same year, combined the previous societies. The Society of Friends came in 1947, although their meeting hall was not completed until 1963. William Marriott, engineer to the Midland and Great Northern Railway, built Brook Hall for use by the Brethren, who formerly met in what is now the Good Companions Club premises in Cremer Street.

The Baptists arrived officially in 1930, the inaugural service being held on 26th February. Previously the congregation had met in a private house in Cromer Road before moving to Cossey Hall in Cremer Street until the present church in Holway Road was opened in 1952. It was extended in 1962 and summer services are now so popular that they have to be moved to the High School Hall in order to accommodate all those who come to worship.

Members of Beeston Road Methodist Church, about 1900.

The Roman Catholic church was designed by Sir Giles Gilbert Scott and was dedicated in 1902. It is the only listed building in Sheringham.

One religious body that has contributed much to the town is the Salvation Army. They were already well established in Grimsby by the 1880s and when local fishermen returned from that port they brought with them an enthusiasm for setting up their own robust form of evangelism. They had no money to build a hall and began to meet in Emery's net loft on Lifeboat Plain in 1888. They were not greeted too enthusiastically by the townspeople and suffered many a broken window and the discourtesy of having a horse and cart driven through one of their outdoor meetings. They were also banned from meeting on the promenade. Perseverance, however, paid off and they opened their hall in Cremer Street in 1896. Their 'Drunk Raids', with band marching through the streets of the town at closing time followed by inebriated citizens, and lasses selling the *War Cry*, became familiar sights in the town. Their work received official recognition in 1910 when General Booth visited the town. Today their uniforms, music and meetings are popular with residents and visitors alike, contributing much to the spiritual and cultural life of the town.

The earlier reference to a 'large number' of private lodging houses was certainly no exaggeration, for White's directory of 1896 lists no fewer than 114 such premises, including that owned by John William Warby, paper miller of Beeston Road. He utilised the water flowing in the Beck, which still flows down to the beach. His works were situated at the lower end of The Avenue at its junction with Beeston Road.

The writer of an article in the *Eastern Daily Press* in October the same year records, rather condescendingly, that the fishermen 'seemed decent fellows', that Jarrold's 'smart shop' (now the site of the Little Theatre coffee shop and bar) marked the place where 'old and new Sheringham unite' and that he was unable to obtain any soda water at the Temperance Hotel in Lower Sheringham (now the Two Lifeboats hotel)!

But before we launch into the new century let us look for a moment at the Sheringham known to young Ann West, later to become mother of Stanley Craske the late local historian to whom I am indebted for much help and guidance in preparing this booklet. There were a few cottages round Beeston Common and the original Dunstable Arms public house offered hospitality on the Cromer Road. There was nothing at all until you turned into what is now Station Road and came across some fishermen's cottages on a site opposite what is now New Road. Below these there were a few more cottages, some shops in Wyndham Street and cottages immediately south of the Two Lifeboats Coffee House, which had been established in 1870. A small bridge connected Wyndham Street to Woodhouse Lane (now Cliff Road) while Beeston Road was no more than an unmade track known as Mill Lane. Co-operative Street did not exist, except as a muddy lane leading to a farm and pond, with no connection through to Beeston Road. Ann drew water from the Polk for her grandmother and from the reservoir at the Town Clock for her mother.

Around the turn of the century there were 'at least 100 boats' working full-time off the beach. Such a number created congestion on the beach and ensuing

In the first half of the 20th century bell tents on the beach were replaced by a new type of canvas tent that could be put up for the season. Visitors could rent them for the day or week.

arguments and frustrations were not helped when incoming boats could not land and be made secure. Some, indeed, were lost and it was against this background that many families decided to seek new lives elsewhere with the years 1904–1908 seeing them settling in such places as Wells, Grimsby, Mablethorpe, Scarborough and Skegness.

Older fishermen recall the old lifeboat house on Lifeboat Plain with its doors opening onto a slipway that went out between the Crown Inn and a private house known as the 'Mo' (called after a daughter of the family who lived there) and onto the beach. This arrangement continued until the construction of the nearby breakwater made launching dangerous and the lifeboat returned to its shed at the Hythe. The lifeboat house was also home to a reading room and Fishermen's Club until about 1914. The Mo was demolished after World War 2, the site then being used as an open-air bandstand and a children's playground. When Anglian Water provided a multi-million pound sewerage scheme for the town they acquired the site from the North Norfolk District Council and in return built an 'amenity building' on the top of a massive storm and overflow tank. This building has remained empty since its construction and negotiations are in progress to convert it into a new museum for Sheringham, to house the Museum Trust's unique collection of historic lifeboats and fishing boats together with the content of the existing town museum.

Where the 'Chequers' car park now is (next to the Shannocks Hotel) there was a collection of cottages known as Tantivy Square, the passageway between the southern wall of the car park and the row of cottages fronting Gun Street being known as Tantivy Loke.

Fishermen and lifeboatmen in front of the Henry Ramey Upcher lifeboat, about 1913. All the names were recorded by local historian Stanley Craske and are available at Sheringham museum.

Sea defences

Changes in the ancient parish of Sheringham took place on 1st October 1901 when it was split into the Urban District of Sheringham (taking in part of Beeston Regis) and the civil parishes of Upper Sheringham and Beeston Regis. The population of the town was then 2,359, that of Beeston Regis 69 and Upper Sheringham 325.

Although the heart of the old town lies round the Wyndham Street/Gun Street/Lifeboat Plain area, there have been other centres in times past and a long history of land losses due to storms and erosion. The encroachment by the sea is a continuing saga for towns such as Sheringham and represents a battle that can never be completely won. The first Crown Inn slid into the sea in October 1800, to be followed by its successor less than 80 years later. The Sheringham Inclosure map of 1811 shows a considerable amount of land to the seaward of the Two Lifeboats Coffee House. This stretched as far west as some cottages fronting what is now Fishermen's Gangway and was known as The Green. For many years, before land and properties disappeared into the sea, it was the site of an annual fair, which subsequently moved to Beeston Common. More cottages and sheds went into the sea in 1877 and in August 1912 torrential rain and overflowing rivers and becks led to much of the town being under water and large losses of cliff at the west end. A further estimated 3,000 tons of cliff at the east end dropped into the sea in 1928.

One of the first duties therefore of the new Urban District Council, who met once a month in the old Post Office building in Church Street (now Bertram Watts, the bookseller), was to look at the town's sea defences. By 1904 they were spending more than £1,800 a year and although there have been exceptional years since then the average loss of land to the sea has been in the region of three feet a year.

The progress of providing sea defences to the town can be seen in the 'stepped' pattern of the promenade and sea-wall. As each length has been completed so the sea has scoured out the unprotected land at either end. With the chalk level of the beach dropping and exposing the base of the wall urgent action was required to prevent further deterioration. The answer was to bring in massive chunks of Norwegian rocks to protect the sea wall by dissipating the power of the waves before they hit it and to prevent beach material being picked up and thrown against it. At Beeston Regis a wooden revetment has been built along the beach to provide some protection to the vulnerable cliffs, for it had been estimated that if the former rate of loss continued the church could have been in the sea by the year 2129. The possibility of this happening led the parishioners, in 1950, to urge the Parochial Church Council to start a fund to either build a new church or re-erect the existing one further inland.

Part of Sheringham seafront, 1981. The 19th-century village of Lower Sheringham is still found in this picture and a bit further to the west, among the 20th-century buildings. The Crown and the Two Lifeboats can be seen in this picture. Today the promenade is further protected by substantial granite blocks placed there at the end of the 20th century.

Entertainment

The town's first cinema, later known as the 'Casino', opened in 1914 in what is now the Masonic Centre on the Cromer Road. The first 'talkies' came to the Regent Hall (on the corner of Cromer Road and Holway Road) in the 1930s. A third cinema, 'The Picture House', originally known as the Town Hall because of its use for public meetings, was taken over by the owners of the Regent in 1958, renamed 'The Empire', and closed in 1960. It was then taken over by the Urban District Council and reopened later that year as the Little Theatre. The Regent closed in December of the same year and now provides accommodation for offices and a social club.

Another place of entertainment was the 'Arcade Lawn' in Church Street, approached up the arcade in the row of shops facing Augusta Street. This was used mainly by summer concert parties and attracted such notable artists as Leslie Henson, Clarkson Rose and Clapham and Dwyer. Despite such patronage it was fairly basic with a covered stage and corrugated iron canopy over the first few rows, the remainder of the seats, on the gravel floor, being totally open to the weather, although a canvas roof was provided later. Mr Bob Rushmer has remembered the wash-house windows of cottages in Station Road overlooking the stage and he enjoyed many a free performance while perched precariously on a chair or copper top. It was also common practice for local children to sit on the pavement edge and watch the 'toffs' pass by in their elegant evening dresses and dinner suits on their way from their luxury accommodation at the Grand, the

Local historian Stanley Craske recorded that about 1900 stylish rigs like this would be brought to the town on railway carriages by the gentry when they came to stay.

The cottage in Whitehall Yard where the Zeppelin dropped its bomb in 1915.

Burlington and the Sheringham Hotel to this rather down-market but popular centre of entertainment.

The outbreak of World War 1 effectively prevented any further development, although the town did achieve its moment in history as the first place in Britain to be bombed from a Zeppelin. This occurred at 8.30pm on 19th January 1915 when the Zeppelin L4 dropped two incendiary bombs on the town, one falling on waste land in Priory Road and the other hitting a cottage in Whitehall Yard off Wyndham Street. It passed through the roof, bedroom ceiling and floor to land on the kitchen floor just behind a chair on which a visitor was sitting. She was slightly injured and the (fortunately unexploded) bomb was taken outside and put into a bucket. The core of the bomb and other memorabilia can be seen in the town's museum. Zeppelins were, in fact, a reasonably common sight along the east coast. The R101 was off the coast in the 1930s and during the years 1938–39 German airship companies operated a suspiciously large number of 'trips' up and down this stretch of coast. Many observers believed their main objective was to check radio wavelengths used in our early radio direction finding stations – the forerunners of our modern, sophisticated radar/early warning systems.

The Regis Silver Fox Farm in Sheringwood is believed to have been established in the late 1920s but by 1933 it had proved to be an unviable project. The answer – to expand into a zoo! The press called it 'the Norfolk Whipsnade', and with its crocodiles, lions, seals, timber wolves, birds of paradise, snakes and pelicans it proved a popular attraction until it closed down on the outbreak of World War 2.

Flint picking

Although the holiday trade was important to the town there was another industry which was also of great benefit to many local people, providing winter employment for fishermen and their families. This was the picking of flints from the beach for milling down and use as body ingredients in the pottery industry in Stoke-on-Trent. The *Eastern Daily Press*, in a contributor's report dated 3rd April

1933, recorded 'men, women and children putting the grey pebbles into baskets and boxes of all sorts and kinds and trundling them along the esplanade in trucks, perambulators and other vehicles'. At that time some 4,500 tons of boulder (blue) flints were being removed every winter, the pickers being paid 6s 6d a ton and the District Council ploughing back some £850, equivalent to a sixpenny rate, into the General Rate Fund.

Work stopped during the war years and it was not until 1960 that picking recommenced when up to 2,500 tons were removed every winter, the District Council receiving the enhanced rate of 11s 6d a ton. Many local people, however, felt this practice was detrimental to the sea defences of the town and after several unsuccessful attempts they finally persuaded the UDC, in April 1969, to cease the practice altogether.

War years

Those who did not know this area of Norfolk during the Second World War can be forgiven for believing Sheringham slumbered quietly as a small coastal resort free from the excitement and drama experienced by other places. In fact, in common with many other Norfolk towns (Cromer, Caister and Great Yarmouth, for example), Sheringham, for its size, saw a great deal of activity. There were numerous air raids and a heavy concentration of troops became a way of life for its inhabitants.

Troops were billeted in the many large, empty, summer houses owned by rich families who summered here every year. Hotels were requisitioned, tents appeared on The Leas, and 6-inch naval guns were sited on Skelding Hill, although never fired in anger because practice shots disturbed the stability of the cliffs! Machine gun posts and pill boxes appeared on the promenade and approach roads to the town. Allied and enemy planes crashed on the beaches and surrounding countryside; roads were closed to civilian traffic; death and destruction came in the 13 air raids on the town (14 killed and 38 'officially' injured) while hundreds of properties suffered varying degrees of damage.

During the early days of the war North Norfolk was subjected to 'tip and run' raids as enemy aircraft sought to test air defences. Later, as raids were extended to

Damage in Barford Road from bombing on 22nd September 1940

inland targets, bombs were dropped to lighten loads on return journeys to bases. The whole area was very much a training ground for thousands of troops, many of them passing through the anti-aicraft training camp at nearby Weybourne (now home of the Muckleburgh Collection and a 'must' for anyone interested in military history and vehicles). They were also a large readily mobilised force in case of any threatened invasion. (The story of wartime Sheringham is told in a companion Poppyland book, *Coastal Towns at War* by the same author.)

Revolutionary plan

Post-war plans for the town were in full swing by 1946, when the UDC bought the present Recreation Ground from Sir Henry Upcher for £2,300 and there was talk of providing chalets on the cliffs, a swimming pool, boating lake, sun shelters and conference hall, as well as a boating lake on Beeston Common. There was also some discussion on the possibility of building a jetty. 'Downtide' West opened a crab processing factory producing 100 per cent pure potted crab paste. The company closed in 1982.

The possibility of a warship visiting the town was also raised. As one councillor said, 'If Cromer can have one why not Sheringham?' Why not indeed. England's first helicopter mail service flew an inaugural flight to Beeston Common in May 1948, finding yet another use for this popular area. Known alternatively as Sheringham Heath and Goose Green, it has long been a playground for the people of the town. Once boasting a three-hole golf course, it has served as a site for travelling fairs and circuses, seen celebration bonfires, been the home of wild orchids, the venue for countless youngsters to play games, hunt for frog-spawn and newts and, for their elders, an area on which simply to stroll and enjoy the scenery. It was designated a Site of Special Scientific Interest in March 1965 and a farsighted management plan resulted, in 1999, in the site being awarded the European honour of being designated a Special Area of Conservation. Local claims that it is one of the best such sites in the county are backed by the knowledge that it is home to over 400 different flowering plants, 14 varieties of orchid and some rare ferns. There are guided walks during the summer months but always the problems caused by inconsiderate dog owners who leave bags of excreta in bushes and alongside paths.

An article in the *Norfolk Chronicle* in February 1919 on 'The Future of Sheringham' referred to the fact that 85 per cent of the townspeople gained their livelihood from visitors and expressed the need for a Winter Garden as somewhere for people to go when the weather was bad. A call was also made for a second golf course for beginners, although there was already a second 18-hole course (now 9 holes) at West Runton.

This plea for extra facilities found a resounding echo in a revolutionary plan for the town published in 1950. This envisaged the 'reconstruction' of an area stretching from the West Cliff and promenade up to New Road, bounded by Beeston Road and High Street and taking in Wyndham Street, Gun Street, and Co-operative Street. Only a bank, butcher's and chemist's shop and the Robin Hood public house would remain. The heart of the town, including the Clock Tower, was to be demolished and replaced by a combination of shops, boarding and apartment houses, conference hall, theatre, winter gardens, dance hall, ice-skating rink, exhibition hall and assembly rooms, municipal offices, hotel, fishing industry buildings, library and art gallery, covered swimming pool, restaurant and bandstand. On the Cromer Road it was planned to build a further pavilion and restaurant, squash courts, covered tennis courts, sports hall and gymnasium. No doubt the plan was prompted by the post-war enthusiasm to sweep away all that

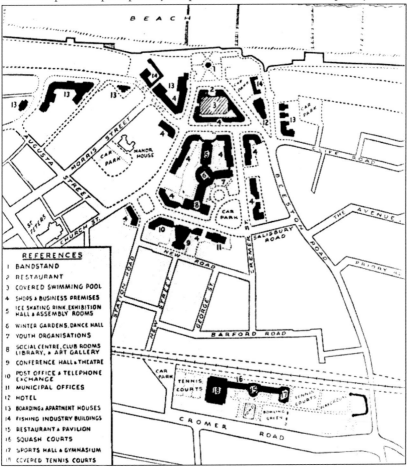

REFERENCES

1 BANDSTAND
2 RESTAURANT
3 COVERED SWIMMING POOL
4 SHOPS & BUSINESS PREMISES
5 ICE SKATING RINK, EXHIBITION
   HALL & ASSEMBLY ROOMS
6 WINTER GARDENS, DANCE HALL
7 YOUTH ORGANISATIONS
8 SOCIAL CENTRE, CLUB ROOMS
   LIBRARY, & ART GALLERY
9 CONFERENCE HALL & THEATRE
10 POST OFFICE & TELEPHONE
   EXCHANGE
11 MUNICIPAL OFFICES
12 HOTEL
13 BOARDING & APARTMENT HOUSES
14 FISHING INDUSTRY BUILDINGS
15 RESTAURANT & PAVILION
16 SQUASH COURTS
17 SPORTS HALL & GYMNASIUM
18 COVERED TENNIS COURTS

The proposed plan for Sheringham in 1950.

was old and replace it with something new. Thankfully, however, it was never implemented and the wheel came full circle in June 1975 when the Town Council committed itself to town centre conservation.

It seems incredible, however, that at the time an editorial in the *North Norfolk News* could applaud this 'practical and realistic approach to the potent problem of keeping abreast of the times' and at the same time record that such a scheme could be achieved without 'in the smallest degree spoiling the town's existing character and natural beauty'.

The New Sheringham Society was also active in suggesting improvements to the town, putting forward the idea of a new road system, including a new coast road coming off the bend in the road immediately east of the railway bridge at Beeston Regis, joining up with Nelson Road and then swinging down Cliff Road, across Lifeboat Plain, along West Cliff (with the necessary demolitions to make way for the increased traffic) and out to join the Weybourne Road. There was also a suggestion to 'straighten out' Barford Road and New Road. The realignment of the former would have resulted in the demolition of many properties in Melbourne Road, Station Road and Waterbank Road, while the latter was planned to end at a roundabout at the junction of High Street and Station Road, outside the Little Theatre.

The *North Norfolk News* carried letters from visitors complaining of the fouling of streets by dogs – still very much a problem today; many feel that the promenade and beach would be much more attractive and healthier if dogs were banned from them altogether.

The Sheringham Policy Map, approved in January 1975 after consultations between the County Council, North Norfolk District Council and the Town Council, pointed the way to the future growth of the town – more residential development at Beeston Regis, on both sides of Holway Road and on the Cromer Road in Sheringham; a new industrial site to replace the allotments on the Weybourne Road; exchanging the present recreation ground in Holt Road with land at the Priory site at Beeston so that access could be gained through the former to a proposed residential site behind the cemetery and a new site for the proposed Middle School.

The residential development has taken place with none of it (in the author's opinion) making any positive contribution to the appearance of main roads into the town. In particular the opportunity has been lost of creating attractive estates, those that have been built being victims of the modern disease of overbuilding on any given area of land with scant regard for visual attractiveness or personal privacy.

The long awaited new Recreation Ground on the Weybourne Road opened in 1995 providing a pavilion with function room, bar and approved disabled facilities. Sportsmen and women have access to two football pitches, a cricket square, floodlit hard tennis courts and a netball pitch. All are well supported and the ground is also used by the Sheringham Carnival Committee and other local organisations.

On the positive side a planning policy has been implemented slowing down the conversion of large houses into retirement homes for the elderly but greater efforts are still needed to ensure that when town centre premises change hands they continue as shops rather than being converted to office use. The town's Health Centre, built at a cost of £250,000, was opened in September 1981, while in the following year Sheringham won the 'Best Kept Town' Competition, with the judges praising its cleanliness and absence of litter. Would that it was always so! The former Sheringham Hotel has been converted into flats whilst retaining much of its original appearance. The Marble Arch and toilets at the west end have been restored and the Town Council has continued its fight (not always successfully unfortunately) against the proliferation of amusement arcades and take-away food shops. The town clock has been restored. Sheringham Hall has been bought by the National Trust and the town centre has retained its compactness and vitality as an attractive shopping area, due in no small measure to it being in a Conservation Area.

The Preservation Society has continued its watching brief to work for the good of the town and has not been slow to fight development which it has considered detrimental to the town.

The biggest single issue dominating the news in recent years has been dubbed the Supermarket Saga. Everyone seems agreed that Sheringham needs a better supermarket, but where? An ideal site would be within the town centre, but no such site exists. Proposed development on the station car park has provoked strong views, both for and against. Rumours abound of a leading national company having acquired a site on the edge of town but hard facts are not obtainable from anyone. Perhaps when the next edition of this booklet appears we will be a bit wiser!

Attempts to establish a museum in the town go back to the 1960s. In the autumn of 1988 the Town Council established a Museum Subcommittee and on 13th July 1991 the then Chairman, Peter Cox, formally opened this new attraction which has grown into an independent trust with the Town Council as its patron; it is situated in five former fishermen's cottages in Station Road.

Sheringham's claim to be the only place in the world to possess four of its original lifeboats has never been challenged. These are the *J. C. Madge* (the town's last pulling and sailing lifeboat), the *Foresters Centenary* (its first motorised lifeboat), the *Manchester Unity of Oddfellows* (its first offshore lifeboat) and the *Henry Ramey Upcher*, which can be seen in its original shed at the top of the West Slipway. The Sheringham Museum Trust owns the first three plus a collection of locally built fishing boats; all have been recognised as of national importance.

Donkeys no longer grace the beach and the bell tents have gone, but the holiday trade remains just as significant today as it was when this photograph was taken early in the 20th century.

The Norfolk Long Distance Coast Path was opened by HRH Prince Charles on 8th July 1986 and in joining up with the Peddars Way at Holme offers some 87 miles of attractive walking through some of the most outstanding coastline of its kind in Europe with its variety of salt marshes, sand dunes, wide sandy beaches and shingle banks. The local section passes through the site of the former Weybourne Camp to Weybourne Hope and along the beach under the cliffs to Old Hythe before rising through the golf course and along the promenade and up Beeston Hill. It then meets existing paths to Cromer where it joins the Weavers Way.

The holiday trade remains the economic backbone of the town with the overall value of tourism in North Norfolk in 1999 being an estimated £186.4 million; it supports 5,690 jobs.

During the last ten years some 700 new properties have been built and currently (2002) there are 191 outstanding planning permissions. Future emphasis will be on infilling small sites, and the District Council now has the power, where they think appropriate, to insist on higher densities than the applicant may wish. It is unlikely, therefore, that the present population of 7,220 (Beeston Regis 1,160) will change dramatically in the future although property prices may well continue their upward spiral.

The town's Carnival continues to attract thousands of visitors and a new event

Squire Clive Rayment and the Lobster Potties morris troupe entertain with a dance at the 2002 Lobster Potties weekend.

is the 'Potty Festival' held in the first week of July. This started in 1986 as a group of local Morris dancers entered as a team, properly known as a 'side', in the Carnival. The first Festival was held in 1994 and it is now an established event with sides coming to Sheringham from all over the country and abroad.

The North Norfolk Railway goes from success to success and an engineering study has been completed which points to the viability of opening the railway crossing at the top of Station Road to connect with Cromer and Norwich. Research is continuing into sources of funding but steam train trips between Holt and Cromer are coming closer with the ultimate destination being Norwich in the future.

The Sixth Form at the High Schools opened in 1995 and the Millennium Building, opened in 2000, concentrates on the humanities with its library, computers, drama studio and specialist teaching facilities. Plans are in hand to relocate the Edinburgh Road School at Holt here (to be known as the Woodfield School), and the new complex, incorporating the existing primary school, will become a learning centre for some 1,400 students aged from 3 to 18 years. A project to become a specialist art college will depend on future funding.

The primary school, built in 1986, was extended in 1994 and a further extension will allow it to cope with a rising number of pupils. The present (spring

2002) total is 572. The school has received recognition in the government's school achievement awards and the future looks bright.

At the beginning of the 19th century upwards of 200 fishing boats operated from Sheringham's beaches – far too many for safety and harmonious working relationships. Many fishermen simply up-boated and took their families to centres such as Grimsby, Skegness and Great Yarmouth to start new lives. Today there are just 20 boats working from Sheringham and only seven of these are full timers. The total catches attributed to Sheringham during 2001 were 55,860 kg of crabs (valued at £70,689) and 4,024 kg of lobsters (£37,476), with the biggest catches coming in June and July respectively. Although listed under 'Sheringham', these figures include catches made at Cley, Weybourne and East and West Runton.

The problems facing the authorities have remained fairly constant ever since this booklet was first published in 1980 – to maintain the delicate balance between preserving what is left of the old town, providing off-season employment and at the same time catering for all those who come to enjoy Sheringham for what it is – a quiet, attractive, relatively unspoilt seaside town where you can relax and enjoy life removed from most of the pressures of modern life, and where the warmth and friendliness of the local people keeps the community spirit very much alive.

Author's Note: No record of the development of Sheringham can be complete without some reference to the lifeboats and crews who have so unselfishly served the town. Poppyland Publishing and others have told their stories, hence the absence of details in this brief history of the town.

Further reading

Ayers, May, *Memoirs of a Shannock*. Larks Press, 1995.

Ayers, May, *Shannocks in Wartime*. Larks Press, 2001.

Brooks, Peter, *Coastal Towns at War: the Story of Cromer and Sheringham in the Second World War*. Poppyland Publishing, 1988.

Cox, Peter, *The Divided Village: Episodes in the Development of Sheringham, Norfolk*. Courtyard Publishing, 2000.

Cox, Peter, *The Village Becomes a Town: the Transformation of Sheringham, Norfolk, 1890–1910*. Courtyard Publishing, 2001.

Craske, Stanley and Roy, *Sheringham: a Century of Change*. Poppyland Publishing, 1985.

Erroll, A. Campbell, *A History of the Parishes of Sheringham and Beeston Regis*. The author, 1970.

Malster, R. W., *The Sheringham Lifeboats 1838–1981*. Poppyland Publishing, 1981.

Youngman, Russell, *Upper Sheringham, early 1930*. Privately printed.